Credit Card Fraud Detection and Analysis through Machine Learning

Anand Sharma
Yogita Goyal

ELIVA PRESS

ELIVA PRESS

Anand Sharma
Yogita Goyal

At the current state of the world, financial organizations expand the availability of financial facilities by employing of innovative services such as credit cards, Automated Teller Machines (ATM), internet and mobile banking services. Besides, along with the rapid advances of e-commerce, the use of credit card has become a convenience and necessary part of financial life. Credit card is a payment card supplied to customers as a system of payment. Nowadays, the Credit card usage is increasing day by day for both regular purchases as well as online. In every transaction of credit card, the bank should check the fraud detection. Year after year, the damages inflicted by the credit card fraud problem are growing rapidly. The intention behind these kinds of fraudulence may be obtaining goods without paying, or unauthorized funds from an account. This book is providing an approach for the credit card fraud detection using machine learning. Logistic regression, anomaly detection, and stochastic gradient descent techniques are used in this approach.

Published: Eliva Press SRL
Address: MD-2060, bd.Cuza-Voda, 1/4, of. 21 Chişinău, Republica
Moldova
Email: info@elivapress.com
Website: www.elivapress.com

ISBN: 978-1-952751-42-4

CREDIT CARD FRAUD DETECTION AND ANALYSIS THROUGH MACHINE LEARNING

Authors

1. Dr. Anand Sharma
2. Ms. Yogita Goyal

ABSTRACT

At the current state of the world, financial organizations expand the availability of financial facilities by employing of innovative services such as credit cards, Automated Teller Machines (ATM), internet and mobile banking services. Besides, along with the rapid advances of e-commerce, the use of credit card has become a convenience and necessary part of financial life. Credit card is a payment card supplied to customers as a system of payment. Nowadays, the Credit card usage is increasing day by day for both regular purchases as well as online. In every transaction of credit card, the bank should check the fraud detection. Year after year, the damages inflicted by the credit card fraud problem are growing rapidly. The intention behind these kinds of fraudulence may be obtaining goods without paying, or unauthorized funds from an account. This book is providing an approach for the credit card fraud detection using machine learning. Logistic regression, anomaly detection, and stochastic gradient descent techniques are used in this approach.

LIST OF FIGURES

Fig No.	Figure Caption	Page No.
4.1	Proposed Model	16
4.2	Confusion Matrix	17
5.1	Spyder IDE	20
6.1	Define feature and targets	23
6.2	Histogram Plotting of Features and Target	23
6.3	Correlation Matrix	24
6.4	Classification Report	24
6.5	ROC Curve of LR	25
6.6	Logistic Regression Curve	25
6.7	Precision and Recall Report under Sample Data	26
6.8	ROC Curve for under Sample Data	26
6.9	Outlier Classification	27
6.10	SVM Classification Report	28
6.11	Training Loss in Credit Card Transaction	28

LIST OF ABBREVIATIONS

CCFD	Credit Card Fraud Detection
ML	Machine Learning
LR	Logistic Regression
SGD	Stochastic Gradient Descent
LOF	Local Outlier Factor
SVM	Support Vector Machine
PCA	Principle Component Analysis
FP	False Positive
TN	True Negative
FN	False Negative
TP	True Positive
AUC	Area Under the Curve
ROC	Receiver Operating Characteristics
KNN	K-Nearest Neighbor
CF	Confusion Matrix

1. INTRODUCTION

Visa extortion is a top to bottom extending timeframe for burglary and misrepresentation devoted the utilization of or with respect to a rate card, which incorporate a Visa or charge card, as a false wellspring of expense assortment in an exchange. Misrepresentation is one of the basic moral issues inside the FICO rating card undertaking. The intention might be to advantage chocolates without paying, or to profit unapproved funds from a record or to benefit a couple of sort of supplier. Anticipation and discovery of misrepresentation in frameworks are basic elements which may be to be contemplated so you can avoid fakes and misfortunes in view of deceitful exercises. As per ACNielsen who done see in 2015, broke down that roughly one-tenth of the segment's people is purchasing on line. India's FICO assessment score card base may furthermore additionally have delegated 20 million in the simply finished up 2013-14 money related year - its most stage inside the past 5 years - in accordance with World line India. As the assortment of FICO rating card holders will develop worldwide extensive, the open doors for fraudster additionally will increment.

1.1. Credit Card Fraud

With regards to the cardboard organization industry, misrepresentation might be depicted on the grounds that the developments attempted using undesired elements to increase undeserved prizes, bringing about a quick money related misfortune to the financial contributions industry. Here, we manage the attempts through fraudsters to apply stolen FICO score card and personality data to steal money, devices or administrations. This has realized the business to think of continuously more noteworthy powerful components to battle Mastercard misrepresentation. A machine student that typifies proficient structures is a case of the kind of component.

Unlawful utilization of Visa or its actualities without the comprehension of the proprietor is alluded to as charge card extortion. Diverse FICO rating card extortion traps have a place particularly with 2 associations of utility and social misrepresentation. Application misrepresentation takes locale when, fraudsters apply new playing cards from budgetary foundation or issuing organizations the utilization of phony or distinctive insights. Numerous bundles can be presented by one buyer with one lot of individual data (called duplication extortion) or stand-out individual with indistinguishable data alluded to as distinguishing proof misrepresentation.

Conduct extortion, of course, has four most essential sorts stolen/lost card, mail theft, fake card and card holder never again present misrepresentation. Stolen/lost card extortion happens when fraudsters acquire a Mastercard or get passage to a lost card. Mail burglary extortion happens while the fraudster get a charge card in mail or individual actualities from monetary foundation before

1

achieving to genuine cardholder. In each fake and cardholder not present fakes, Visa data are gotten without the comprehension of card holders. In the previous, far away exchanges can be done the utilization of card data through mail, cellphone, or the Internet. In the last mentioned, fake cards are made fundamentally dependent on card information.

1.2. Elements of Credit Card Fraud

The term FICO rating card extortion is extensively used to counsel the utilization of a charge card, check card, or any comparable state of FICO assessment, to make buys, or to accomplish budgetary preferred standpoint with the expectation of taking off cost. This incorporates recognizable proof burglary, character supposition, and extortion binges. According to the guideline, positive components are required for money related or distinguishing proof burglary wrongdoing to be named a state of FICO assessment card misrepresentation. These incorporate-

- Credit Card Theft - The taking of a credit card, or credit card variety, from any other individual, without the cardholder's consent, with the reason of the usage of or promoting it.
- Credit Card Forgery - The buying of something of cost the usage of a credit card, via a person other than the cardholder, or an authorized person, with the cause of defrauding the cardboard's company.
- Credit Card Fraud - The taking of a credit score card, or credit card quantity, from another person, with the purpose to use, sell, or switch it to every other man or woman, or using the credit card or card range to buy something of fee, with the cause to defraud.

1.3. Types of fraud

Charge card extortion has been isolated into two sorts; Off-line misrepresentation and On-line extortion. Disconnected misrepresentation Offline extortion is submitted by method for utilizing a stolen physical card at name focus or some other area and On-line misrepresentation online extortion is given through web, cellphone, obtaining, net, or without card holder.

There are more sorts of misrepresentation like

- **Theft fraud/counterfeit fraud** - This area moving around theft extortion and fake misrepresentation, which are identified with each other. Burglary misrepresentation approach utilizing a card that isn't forever yours. The miscreant will take the card of an individual else and use it as in numerous occasions as attainable sooner than the cardboard is blocked. The sooner the proprietor will respond and reach the money related organization, the snappier the bank will take measures to avert the hoodlum. So also, fake misrepresentation happens when the Visa is utilized remotely; best the FICO

2

rating card subtleties are wished. At a certain point, one will copy your card assortment and codes and utilize it by means of positive net-sites, where no signature or physical cards are required.

- **Application fraud** - Application extortion is the point at which an individual applies for a charge card with false data. To hit upon application misrepresentation, the appropriate response is to put into impact an extortion gadget that grants making sense of suspicious projects. To hit upon application misrepresentation, two explicit circumstances should be remarkable when applications originated from an equivalent character with the equivalent data, the so-alluded to as copies, and keeping in mind that programs originate from outstanding people with comparative subtleties, the so alluded to as personality fraudsters.

1.4.Credit Card Fraud Detection Techniques

In this way, exactly what does misrepresentation recognition involve? Misrepresentation recognition is the demonstration of distinguishing deceitful conduct when it happens, which contrasts from extortion anticipation where systems are send With card backers always planning to expand their activities by methods for propelling forceful crusades to advantage greater bits of the market extent, the utilization of time has end up being increasingly more across the board in making it less troublesome for individuals to execute and spend. This development in simplicity of spending through the use of age has, unfortunately, also outfitted a stage for will increment in fake action. Misrepresentation levels have in this manner forcefully risen on the grounds that the 1990's, and the expansion in Visa extortion is costing the card supplier industry really billions of dollars to make it increasingly more difficult for individuals to submit misrepresentation inside the primary spot. One ought to expect that the statute of counteractive action is superior to anything treatment may need to in addition be triumphant appropriate here; yet as noted in the first subsection, aversion isn't generally sufficiently compelling to downsize the unreasonable extortion rate that torment the FICO assessment card association thus persuading the sending of misrepresentation discovery instruments . As preparing vitality will build, extortion recognition itself may likewise even come to be a counteractive action approach inside what's to come. The way that financial assessment rating playing cards are connected in out of control situations, and because of the truth genuine card holders may furthermore moreover charming comprehend that they've been taken addition of weeks after the genuine extortion occasion, makes FICO score playing cards a smooth and wanted focus for misrepresentation.. A great deal of money might be stolen in a brisk time, leaving truly no trace of the fraudster. Distinguishing misrepresentation as fast as reasonable after it happens is in this way fundamental to offer the card association a threat to as a base limit the damage. As fast as an exchange is hailed as a plausible extortion, the cardboard holder might be called to establishment whether or not the exchange altered into legitimate or never again and the cardboard blocked if basic. Misrepresentation examination and the chargeback procedure are exceptionally valued and situated some of weight on assets. The snappier extortion can be distinguished the better; however the tremendous amount of records required now and again piles of exchanges as indicated by 2d - makes constant discovery intense and once in a while even infeasible. Numerous banks attempt and discover misrepresentation as speedy as plausible after it go off, as opposed to recognizing it in real time, as a result of reality extortion location would gradual be able to down an authorization solicitation to such a degree, that it times out.

The Mastercard misrepresentation identification methods are arranged in renowned classes' extortion assessment (abuse discovery) and individual conduct assessment (oddity location).

The main business of strategies offers with administered class task in exchange degree. In these systems, exchanges are arranged as fake or normal dependent on past noteworthy data. This dataset is then used to make arrangement models which could are anticipating the nation (standard or misrepresentation) of new insights. There are various rendition presentation strategies for an in vogue class characterization challenge together with principle acceptance, choice shrubberies and neural systems. This method is analyzed to dependably hit upon most misrepresentation rules, it furthermore alluded to as abuse location.

The second system manages unsupervised procedures which can be founded on record conduct. In this methodology an exchange is recognized deceitful if it's miles in appraisal with clients ordinary direct. This is due to the fact we don't anticipate fraudsters behave just like the account owner or be privy to the behavior version of the owner .To this aim, we want to extract the valid consumer behavioral version for every account and then stumble on fraudulent sports activities in line with it. This approach is also referred to as anomaly detection.

1.5. Machine Learning

Machine learning is a subfield of manmade brainpower. Machine learning alludes to a framework that can naturally enhance with past involvement. In ML programming can hold the capacity to gain from past perception to make derivation about both future conduct and also in forthcoming situations. It is factual based learning approach.

Learning is any procedure by which a framework enhances execution by encounter. As insight require information, it is important to PC to procure learning. There are three types of Machine Learning -

- **Supervised Learning-** Utilizes a progression of named case with coordinate input. Find design in the information with known target class or mark. This example are then use to anticipate the estimation of target quality in future information cases.
- **Unsupervised Learning** – There is no criticism .There is no objective property. Class names of the information are obscure. On the off chance that there is a given arrangement of information, the errand is to build up the presence of classes or groups in the information
- **Reinforcement Learning** - There is backhanded criticism. It is near human learning Algorithm takes in a strategy the proper behavior in a given situation. Each activity has some effect in the earth, and the earth gives compensates that aides the learning calculation. Support learning is the issue looked by a specialist that learns conduct through experimentation connections with a dynamic situation.

There is different type of models of machine learning like Decision tree classifier, Gaussian naïve-bayes, linear and logistic Regression, k-nearest neighbor, Ensemble methods.

1.5.1 Decision Trees
Decision Trees are a form of Supervised Machine Learning (that is you give an explanation for what the input is and what the corresponding output is within the schooling records) in which the data is constantly split in keeping with a sure parameter. The tree can be explained through two entities, specifically decision nodes and leaves.

1.5.2 Gaussian naïve bayes
Naive Bayes classifiers are a set of classification algorithms primarily based on Bayes' Theorem. It isn't a unmarried set of rules but a family of algorithms where they all share a not unusual principle, i.e. Every pair of features being labeled is unbiased of each different.

1.5.3 Regression
Regression is a statistical size used in finance, making an investment and other disciplines that attempts to determine the energy of the relationship among one based variable (generally denoted by Y) and a chain of other converting variables (known as impartial variables). Regression allows funding and monetary managers to fee assets and recognize the relationships among variables, which includes commodity fees and the stocks of businesses dealing

in the ones commodities.

1.5.4 K-nearest neighbor
K-Nearest Neighbors is one of the maximum basic yet important type algorithms in Machine Learning. It belongs to the supervised getting to know area and finds severe software in sample reputation, statistics mining and intrusion detection. It is extensively disposable in actual-life scenarios since it is non-parametric, meaning, it does now not make any underlying assumptions approximately the distribution of data.

1.6. Objective
The objective of the work is to analyze the existing algorithm (Logistic Regression) and to propose a new model of fraud detection.

1.7. Motivation
Every year, card guarantors endure monstrous financial misfortunes because of card extortion and, in this way, huge holes of money can be spared if a triumph and incredible misrepresentation location procedures are connected. There are a few unique factors that make card extortion inquire about beneficial .While card misrepresentation misfortunes against generally speaking turnover have unquestionably declined inside the previous decade or somewhere in the vicinity - totally because of card backers effectively. The greatest evident increase of getting a legitimate misrepresentation recognition machine in area is the limit and oversees of ability monetary misfortune because of deceitful intrigue.

1.8. Book Outline
This book details about the analysis of credit card fraud detection. The book is consisting of six chapters starting with the introductory knowledge about the credit card fraud detection and ending with the last chapter that is conclusion and future work.

- Chapter-1 states the introductory knowledge about the research field and motivation of the work.

- Chapter-2 discusses the related work done in past few years.

- Chapter-3 studies the methodology and learning algorithms which we use in research.

- Chapter-4 illustrates the design of implementation or proposed model that has been carried out.

- Chapter-5 describes the tool which used in implementation

- Chapter-6 contains the experimental results.

2. LITERATURE SURVEY

This chapter determines the literature survey of credit card fraud detection. The previous work on credit card fraud detection is being studied and is being documented in this chapter.

In [1], N. Malini et al. Mention that the anomaly location strategy principally dependent on unsupervised learning is wanted to recognize FICO assessment card misrepresentation over exception directed picking up information of, on the grounds that unsupervised picking up learning of anomaly does now not require past actualities to mark measurements as deceitful. In this way, it needs to learn by methods for the utilization of ordinary exchanges to separate among a lawful offense or unlawful exchange. exception discovery is some other technique used to find both managed and unsupervised becoming acquainted with. Managed anomaly identification method contemplates and characterizes the exception utilizing the preparation dataset. On the other hand, unsupervised exception discovery is much similar to grouping data into different partnerships essentially dependent on their qualities.

In [2] Sridhar Ramawamy et al. describe A few procedures have been proposed for anomaly location dependent on outstanding suspicions and methods. For Gaussian dispersion we can either form every one of the properties together as one multivariate appropriation or with the guide of displaying each characteristic as a different Gaussian conveyance. One of the most extreme not unordinary and natural ways to deal with discover exceptions is by method for expecting a basic dissemination for the records.

In [3], John O. Awoyemi et al. described other typically utilized techniques depend absolutely on the hole measure nearest neighbor procedures have been utilized to unearth anomalies with this presumption. . In this procedure it's far expected that everyone standard records guides lie close toward one another and exceptions are far from them.

Another methodology is bunching based thoroughly approach wherein it is accepted that typical measurements focuses make groups and irregularities are both no longer piece of any group or make separate bunches. To triumph over this issue, sub space grouping is finished with a supposition that every one of the subspaces is hub parallel to reduce the unpredictability of investigating subspaces. Nonetheless, data much of the time make distinctive groups for unprecedented arrangement of characteristics and these bunch lie in one of a kind subspaces.

Chandola et al.[4] spread a more prominent extensive study on related artistic creations inside the subject of anomaly identification and grouping in high dimensional records. As of late outfit of unsupervised strategies is utilized for exception location.

Charu C et al. [5] Portray Ensemble is built up to be more powerful than a solitary methodology and is intensely utilized in directed putting However, utilization of gathering in unsupervised setting and for anomaly identification has its very own requesting circumstances and isn't constantly considered as great as the use of group for regulated setting.

Zimek et al. [6] separated research to merge the work achieved the utilization of gatherings for exception recognition and featured the requesting circumstances identified with it.

Snehal Patil et al. [7] portrays the "Choice Tree Induction Algorithm" that is utilized for Credit Card Fraud Detection. Charge card extortion location is to diminish the bank dangers, widely used to level the exchange data with Visa misrepresentation exchange of authentic profile test to expect the likelihood of being deceitful for another transaction. In this paper it examines roughly the methodology, decision tree approach is another expense delicate methodology contrasted and acclaimed customary sort models on a genuine world Mastercard extortion records set, which decreases the aggregate of misclassification cost even as choosing the part trademark at each non-terminal hub is predominant. Dr R.Dhanapal, Gayathiri. P [8], portrays the "Mastercard Fraud Detection Using Decision Tree for following IP Address Email. By the utilization of this methodology, we can ready to discover the fake customer/specialist organization through the phony mail, following, IP address. On the off chance that the mail is fake, the client/vendor is suspicious and records about the proprietor/sender is followed by means of IP manage.

Raghavendra Patidar, Lokesh Sharma[12] depicts the "Neural Network" is utilized for the assessment on one way answer by means of utilizing neural system, for coordinating the past put away examples and by and by utilized styles from which we will find such examples for Credit Card Fraud Detection.

Yogesh Bharat Sonawane, et al. [13] portrays the "Grouping Based Approach" with K- implies bunch assessment is a route for crushing dataset down into described parts in one of these way that examples and request will wind up discernible. Looking exceptions is a top notch obligation in alright strategy bunching for Credit Card Fraud Detection.

Mr. P. Matheswaran, et al.[14] portrays the "Information Mining Techniques" for Fraud Detection in Credit Card. They hit upon the shrouded records like whether an approaching exchange is deceitful or not. They moreover isolating the exchange sum in three classes utilized on unique degrees of exchange sum each gathering demonstrate the distortion images. The stand-out strides in charge card exchange preparing are spoken to on the grounds that the basic stochastic arrangement of a Hidden Markov Model. Gee is utilized to adaptation the grouping of activity in FICO rating card exchanges with the lead of cardholder.

K. Rama Kalyani, D.Uma Devi [15] depicts the "Hereditary Algorithm is the strategy of discovering best response for the issue and verifiably create the outcomes utilizing hereditary arrangement of tenets, In this paper we utilize Genetic Algorithm for Detecting the misrepresentation of Credit Card Payment System by utilizing the likelihood of extortion exchanges that can be anticipated not long after Mastercard exchanges with the guide of the banks.

Siddhartha Bhattacharyya, et al.[16] Two propelled measurements mining procedures, guide and arbitrary backwoods, vector machines together with the well-known calculated relapse, as a piece of an endeavor to higher find (and as needs be oversee and arraign) financial assessment card extortion. The take a gander at is essentially founded on genuine ways of life records of exchanges from a worldwide FICO assessment task card. It is legitimately comprehended, smooth to apply, and stays one of the greatest regularly utilized for records-mining in exercise.

Suman and Nutan et al. [17] the false exchanges are the ones especially perceived with the guide of the institutional reviewers as the individuals who expedited an illicit exchange of funds from the budgetary organization supporting the credit playing a game of cards. These exchanges were observed to be fake disclose.

Adrian Banarescu [18] depicts the "Distinguishing and Preventing Fraud with Data Analytics". Extortion involves comprehensively immense money related dangers which can likewise undermine benefit, and the image of a budgetary substance. An audit, the period might be completed to improve misrepresentation aversion and discovery, internal of an open or individual financial element.

Aman Srivastava [19] portrays the charge card misrepresentation discovery at Merchant Side the utilization of Neural Networks. Extortion identification the use of neural network is certainly founded absolutely on the human mind running generally essential. Neural system period has made a PC ready to assume. As human mind inquire about by means of past appreciate and utilize its learning or revel in settling on the decision stuck in an unfortunate situation the equivalent technique is executed with the charge card extortion recognition age.

2.1. Research Gap

People are using credit card payment for bill payment, shopping, online transaction has considerably increased in number and gradually there is an increase in fraud transactions as well. We should avoid the fraud transaction which would raise by a fraudster form the detection purpose there are so many detection techniques. The detection techniques is mostly based on the methods like Clustering techniques, Hidden Markov Model, Decision Tree, Neural Networks and, these are evolved in detecting the various credit card fraudulent transactions. While credit card fraud detection has gained wide-scale attention in the literature, there are yet some issues (a number of significant open issues) that face researchers and have not been addressed before adequately such as nonexistence of standard algorithm.

3. METHODOLOGIES USED

In this section we will discuss the methodology for evaluation and metrics. Algorithms are also included in this section. So for credit card fraud detection we use logistic regression with stochastic gradient descent and anomaly detection methods.

3.1. Logistic Regression

Firstly, what is regression, so regression is basically a method for figuring out the statistical relationship among or extra variables where a exchange in a established variable is related to, and relies upon on, a exchange in a single or extra impartial variables. Statistical technique to forecasting trade in a based variable (sales revenue, for instance) on the idea of alternate in a single or more independent variables (population and earnings, as an example) known as curve becoming or line becoming due to the fact a regression analysis equation may be used in fitting a curve or line to records points, in a way such that the variations inside the distances of facts factors from the curve or line are minimized. Relationships depicted in a regression evaluation are, but, associative only, and any motive-impact (causal) inference is solely subjective additionally called regression method or regression method.

There are two types of regression

- **Linear regression** -Linear regression is a basic and generally used form of predictive assessment. The normal idea of regression is to take a look at two topics- first is does a hard and fast of predictor variables do an extraordinary challenge in predicting a final consequences (based) variable? Second is which variables especially are extensive predictors of the very last outcomes variable, and in what manner do they indicated by means of the fee and sign of the beta estimates impact the final results variable? These regression estimates are used to explain the relationship among one based totally variable and one or greater unbiased variables. The best shape of the regression equation with one structured and one impartial variable is defined through the technique $y = c + b*x$, wherein y = anticipated based variable rating, c = consistent, b = regression coefficient, and x = score at the independent variable.

- **Logistic Regression** – Logistic regression is the ideal regression assessment to behavior while the established variable is dichotomous (binary). Like all regression analyses, the logistic regression is a predictive assessment. Logistic regression is used to explain information and to offer an cause of the relationship between one established binary variable and one or extra nominal, ordinal, c program language period or ratio-level unbiased variables.

Calculated relapse is utilized to are envisioning the binomial (Yes/No, 1/0, etc)

12

last outcomes of a response (introduced) variable utilizing one or a few indicator (unbiased) factors as noticeable above. The indicators can be binomial, specific, or numerical. As in a few straight relapse, we need a component that interfaces the fair-minded factors to the built up factor. Anyway the essential qualification directly here is that the based variable can best handle two qualities Yes/No or 1/0. So we need a strategy to outline non-avoid capacity of unbiased factors to a paired result. We in addition need an approach to score the paired absolute last outcomes to choose the likelihood of a "Yes" or "No" result.

In the charge card dataset there might be superb ness 0 or 1, tastefulness 0 for non-false exchange and class 1 for fake exchange and v1-v28 is PCA exchanges.

Initial Step - With the calculated response include or logit trademark, map the consistent indicators to a capacity (the logit) of the reaction variable, which is moreover constant. Utilizing the above example, the indicators can frame a direct capacity together with

$$\text{Logit(Class?)} = b + b1*v1 + b2*v2 + b3*v3 + b4*v4 + \ldots\ldots\ldots + b28*v28$$

This may tackle any fee from -Infinity to +Infinity

Second Step - Convert the logit into odds. This is straightforward due to the truth logit isn't always something however the logarithm of odds of the reaction variable.

$$\text{Log (odds(Class?))} = \text{Logit(Class?)}$$

This will simplest be terrific valued- from 0 to +Infinity

Third Step - Once we recognize the odds, we understand the hazard rating. Probability p,

$$p = \text{odds}/(1+\text{odds})$$

This may also additionally satisfactory be valued from 0 to 1.

If you set up a cutoff fee alongside 0.5, then we take into account that a response is a "Yes" for all ratings above the cutoff and vice-versa for predictive an splendid model.

3.2. Anomaly Detection for outlier detection

Anomaly detection is a way used to perceive uncommon patterns that do not conform to anticipated conduct, referred to as outliers. It has many packages in enterprise, from intrusion detection (identifying atypical patterns in network traffic that might signal a hack) to system health monitoring (spotting a malignant tumor in an MRI test), and from fraud detection in credit score rating card transactions to fault detection in working environments.

3.3.Stochastic Gradient Descent with LR

Gradient Descent is the approach of minimizing a characteristic with the aid of following the gradients of the cost function. This consists of knowing the form of the rate further to the by-product just so from a given factor you recognize the gradient and can pass in that course, e.g. Downhill closer to the minimum price.

- **Gradient Descent Procedure**

The process starts offevolved off with preliminary values for the coefficient or coefficients for the characteristic. These may be 0.Zero or a small random price.

$$Coefficient = 0.0$$

The fee of the coefficients is evaluated via plugging them into the feature and calculating the rate.

$$Price = f\,(coefficient)$$
$$or$$
$$value = examine\,(f\,(coefficient))$$

The derivative of the charge is calculated. The by-product is a idea from calculus and refers back to the slope of the function at a given factor. We need to apprehend the slope simply so we understand the direction (sign) to move the coefficient values with a purpose to get a lower value on the subsequent generation.

$$delta = derivative(cost)$$

Now that we realize from the spinoff which path is downhill, we will now replace the coefficient values. A learning rate parameter (alpha) must be sure that controls how a excellent deal the coefficients can alternate on every replace. Coefficient = coefficient – (alpha * delta)

This process is repeated until the value of the coefficients (price) is 0.0 or close sufficient to zero to be good enough.

- **Stochastic gradient Descent –**

This way may be used to locate the set of coefficients in a version that result in the smallest mistakes for the version on the schooling statistics. Each technology, the coefficients (b) in gadget mastering language are up to date using the equation-

$$b = b + learning\_rate * (y - yhat) * yhat * (1 - yhat) * x$$

Where b is the coefficient or weight being optimized, learning_rate is a learning price that you must con Figure (e.g. Zero.01), (y – yhat) is the prediction mistakes for the version at the training facts attributed to the weight, yhat is the prediction made thru the coefficients and x is the input fee.

- Learning rate - The length of these steps is called the studying price. With a excessive getting to know charge we are able to cowl extra ground each step, however we hazard overshooting the lowest point because the slope of the hill is continuously changing. With a very low getting to know rate, we will with a bit of luck move in the direction of the bad gradient due to the fact we are recalculating it so often. A low studying price is greater precise, however calculating the gradient is time-ingesting, so it's going to take us a very long term to get to the lowest.

- Cost feature -A Loss Functions tells us "how true" our model is at making predictions for a given set of parameters. The price feature has its very own curve and its personal gradients. The slope of this curve tells us how to replace our parameters to make the version greater correct.

4. PROPOSED WORK

After reviewing previous methods now time to design our proposed approach. In this section we are proposing a new scheme which is combination of anomaly detection and logistic regression with stochastic gradient descent.

4.1. Proposed Model

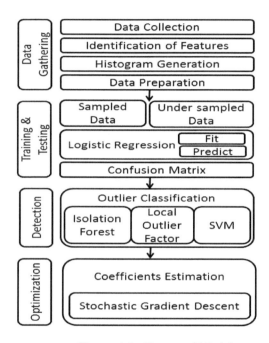

Figure 4.1 : Proposed Model

4.1.1.   *Steps involved in proposed method*

- Data Gathering- Firstly Download python 3.6.5 and Import libraries like Scipy, numpy, matplotlib, pandas, sklearn. Load credit card dataset and identify the features and the target in the data set. And view the histograms of each of the features and fraud class histogram.
- Data preparation Step - Next we prepare the features for the machine learning algorithm. The machine learning algorithm requires standard normally distributed data .
- Training and Testing – In this we applying supervised machine learning

16

Logistic regression model. We split the dataset into training and test set and trains our model. and Train the model using 'fit' method and Test the model using 'predict' method and produce a classification report, an accuracy score, and confusion matrix.

- In confusion matrix we find precision, recall , f1-score , support and find the model accuracy. For 100% success rate for TPs (true positives) and the lowest error rate for FNs (false negatives).Plot the ROC curve and The AUPRC (Area Under the Precision-Recall Curve) that shows the trade-off between precision and recall.
- Again applying this LR method to under sampled data for more accurate result.
- Applying anomaly Detection method- In this we identify classifier outliers like Isolation Forest, Local Outlier Factor and Support Vector Machine .and predict the fraud score.
- Optimization- we apply stochastic gradient descent in logistic regression so that optimize the result accuracy in fraudulent transaction.

4.1.2. Performance Metrics
- **Confusion matrix-** A confusion matrix is a table that is often used to describe the performance of a classification model (or "classifier") on a set of test data for which the true values are known. It allows the visualization of the performance of an algorithm. It allows easy identification of confusion between classes e.g. one class is commonly mislabeled as the other. Most performance measures are computed from the confusion matrix. In the field of machine learning and specifically the problem of statistical classification, a confusion matrix, also known as an error matrix.

	Class 1 Predicted	Class 2 Predicted
Class1 Actual	TP	FN
Class 2 Actual	FP	TN

Figure 4.2 : Confusion Matrix

Here, Class 1 is Positive and Class 2 is Negative.
Meaning of the Terms-
    • Positive (P) - Observation is high caliber (for example is an apple).

• Negative (N) - Observation isn't successful (for instance isn't an apple).

• False Negative (FN) - Observation is sure, yet is foreseen horrible.

• True Positive (TP) - Observation is favorable, and is relied upon to be phenomenal.

• True Negative (TN) - Observation is horrible, and is foreseen to be terrible.

• False Positive (FP) - Observation is poor, anyway is foreseen high caliber.Classification Rate or Accuracy is given via the relation-

$$Accuracy = (TP + TN) / (TP + TN + FP + FN)$$

Classification report visualizer displays the precision, recall, F1, and support scores for the model.

Recall- Recall may be described because the ratio of the whole quantity of correctly classified high exceptional examples divide to the overall range of powerful examples. High Recall indicates the beauty is effectively recognized (small huge type of FN).Recall is given by using the relation-

$$Recall = TP / (TP + FN)$$

Precision- To get the price of precision we divide the entire huge sort of effectively classified awesome examples with the aid of the overall number of anticipated excessive nice examples. High Precision shows an instance classified as satisfactory is genuinely exceptional (small variety of FP). Precision is given by using manner of the relation-

$$Precision = TP / (TP + FP)$$

F-degree- Since we have measures (Precision and Recall) it enables to have a size that represents each of them. We calculate an F-measure which makes use of Harmonic Mean in area of Arithmetic Mean as it punishes the extreme values extra. The F-Measure will always be nearer to the smaller cost of Precision or Recall.

$$F \text{ measure} = (2 * Recall * Precision) / (Recall + Precision)$$

4.1.3.Isolation Forest Algorithm

A standout amongst the most present procedures to find peculiarities is known as Isolation Forests. The arrangement of principles is based at the way that oddities are actualities factors that are not many and novel. As an end final product of those habitations, oddities are inclined to a component known as seclusion.

How Isolation Forests Work - The Isolation Forest arrangement of strategies disengages perceptions by means of haphazardly picking a capacity and after that arbitrarily settling on a separation rate among the most and negligible estimations of the picked capacity. The decision making ability contention is

18

going-separating inconsistency perceptions is less complex on the grounds that just a few conditions are expected to isolate the ones occasions from the conventional perceptions. Then again, keeping separated normal perceptions require more prominent conditions. Subsequently, an irregularity score might be determined because of the reality the scope of conditions required to part a given explanation.

4.1.4.Local Outlier Factor Algorithm-
The LOF algorithm is an unsupervised outlier detection method which computes the local density deviation of a given data issue with recognize to its pals. It considers as outlier samples which have a extensively decrease density than their pals. The variety of acquaintances taken into consideration, (parameter n_neighbors) is commonly chosen
- More than the minimum number of items a cluster has to comprise, simply so special items can be close by outliers relative to this cluster, and
- Smaller than the most range of nearby gadgets that may doubtlessly be nearby outliers.

4.2. About Dataset
The purpose of Dissertation is to implement a device getting to know algorithm to hit upon credit score card fraud based totally on a dataset that carries credit score card transactions made by european cardholders. This dataset consists of transactions that passed off in the route of days in September 2016, with 492 fraudulent transactions out of a total of 284,315 transactions. The dataset is thus enormously unbalanced with the fantastic magnificence (frauds) accounting for simply zero.17% of all transactions. The dataset has 30 enter functions, 28 of which anonymized, and 1 target variable. It includes best numerical enter variables which are the end result of a PCA transformation.. Features V1, V2, ... V28 are the essential additives acquired with PCA, the only functions that have not been transformed with PCA are 'Time' and 'Amount'.
- Feature 'Time' consists of the seconds elapsed among every transaction and the primary transaction in the dataset. The characteristic 'Amount' is the transaction Amount, this selection may be used as an instance-based fee-touchy mastering.
- Feature 'Class' is the response variable and it takes fee 1 in case of fraud and zero otherwise

5. TOOL USED

5.1. Anaconda

With extra than 6 million clients, the open supply Anaconda Distribution is the speediest and maximum handy method to do Python and R insights revolutionary know-how and system becoming acquainted with on Linux, Windows, and Mac OS X. It's the business popular for developing, experimenting with, and training on a solitary framework. Together with a rundown of Python packages, apparatuses like editors, Python circulations consist of the Python translator. Anaconda is used for scientific computing, records technological know-how, statistical evaluation, and system reading. The extremely-current version of Anaconda 5.Zero.1 is launched in October 2017.The launched model five.0.1 addresses some minor insects and presents beneficial capabilities, including updated R language assist. All of those talents weren't available in the genuine five.0.0 launch. This package deal supervisor is also an surroundings manager, a Python distribution, and a group of open supply programs and carries more than a thousand R and Python Data Science Packages.

5.2. Spyder IDE

Spyder is a powerful medical surroundings written in Python, for Python, and designed by way of and for scientists, engineers and facts analysts.

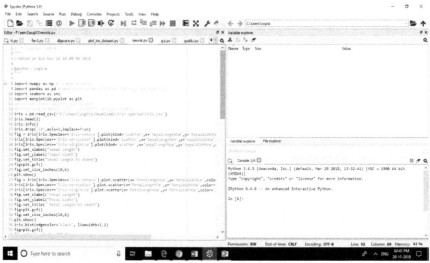

Figure 5.1 : Spyder IDE

20

It capabilities a unique mixture of the superior enhancing, analysis, debugging and profiling functionality of a complete development tool with the facts exploration, interactive execution, deep inspection and exquisite visualization capabilities of a scientific bundle. Furthermore, Spyder gives built-in integration with many popular scientific applications, inclusive of NumPy, SciPy, Pandas, IPython, QtConsole, Matplotlib, SymPy, and extra.

5.3. Python Language
Python is an excessive-level programming language devised with the aid of Guido van Rossum & first released in 1991. It's the most famous coding language utilized by software developers to build, control, manipulate and for testing. In Python, compiled code is saved with the report extension .py For instance new.py . It is likewise an interpreter which executes Python applications. The python interpreter is called python.Exe on Windows. To execute new.py program, kind – python new.py

5.4. Python Packages
Packages or additional libraries help in clinical processing and computational displaying. In Python, the bundles are not a piece of the Python famous library. Barely any significant bundles are
- Numpy-Traditionally, we begin our rundown with the libraries for logical applications, and NumPy is one of the essential bundles around there. It is planned for preparing huge multidimensional clusters and grids, and a broad gathering of abnormal state scientific capacities and actualized techniques makes it conceivable to perform different tasks with these articles.
- Scipy - Another center library for logical processing is SciPy. It depends on NumPy and thusly expands its abilities. SciPy essential records structure is yet again a multidimensional cluster, actualized by Numpy. The package conveys gear that assists with illuminating direct variable based math, chance standard, basic analytics and loads of additional obligations.
- Matplotlib - Another inside library for clinical registering is SciPy. It depends on NumPy and along these lines broadens its abilities. SciPy number one measurements structure is once more a multidimensional cluster, actualized by utilizing Numpy. The bundle consolidates gadget that assistance with settling direct polynomial math, chance statute, crucial analytics and heaps of more noteworthy obligations.
- Pandas - Pandas is a Python library that gives high-organize measurements frameworks and an across the board kind of apparatus for examination. The superb normal for this bundle bargain is the ability to interpret as

21

elective complex activities with insights into one or directions. Pandas consolidate many implicit systems for gathering, sifting, and joining data, notwithstanding the time-arrangement usefulness. The majority of this has gone with by means of astounding pace signs.

- Seaborn - Seaborn is fundamentally a superior stage API based absolutely at the matplotlib library. It joins more noteworthy fitting default settings for handling graphs. Additionally, there is a rich display of representations comprehensive of some confounded kinds like time arrangement, joint plots, and violin diagrams. The seaborn refreshes extensively cover bug fixes.
- Sklearn - Scikit-inquire about presents in excess of a couple of directed and unsupervised learning calculations through a steady interface in Python. It is ensured beneath a lenient improved BSD permit and is dispatched under numerous Linux dispersions, empowering instructional and business use. The library is based upon the SciPy (Scientific Python) that should be built up sooner than you may utilize scikit- investigate.

6. SIMULATION RESULTS

This section contains the performance results of our implementation method. The proposed calculation is actualized in anaconda tool results will be shown below.

6.1. Import the data and libraries and Identify the features and the target in the data set

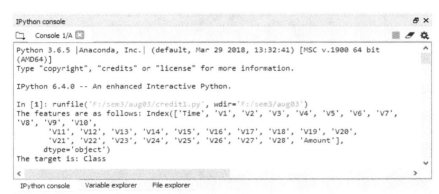

Figure 6.1: Define feature and targets

6.2. Histogram plotting- We see that the unlabeled feature values have been transformed, they're the result of a PCA transformation. Amount isn't and neither is Time.

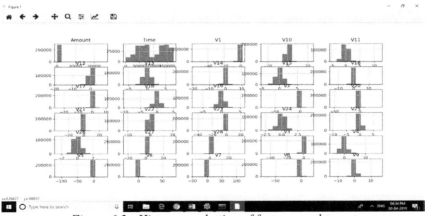

Figure 6.2 : Histogram plotting of features and target

6.3. Plot the correlation matrix

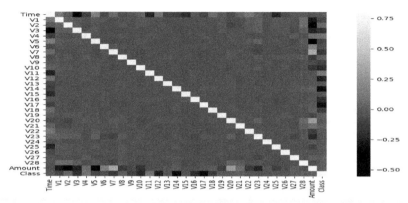

Figure 6.3 : Correlation matrix

The above correlation matrix shows that none of the V1 to V28 PCA components have any correlation to each other however if we observe Class has some form positive and negative correlations with the V components but has no correlation with Time and Amount.

6.4. Performing the logistic Regression Algorithm and .fit and .predict method.

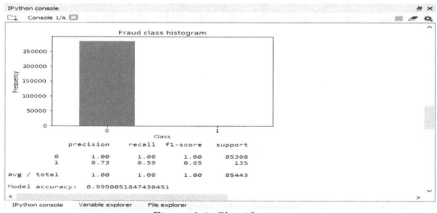

Figure 6.4: Classification report

The dataset we have is drastically biased toward non-fraudulent transactions (284,315) in comparison with fraudulent transactions (492).Accuracy is so high, so model is over fitting, so to reduce it we use under sample data.

6.5. The ROC curve below shows that our model is quite good for detecting true positives and minimizing false positives.

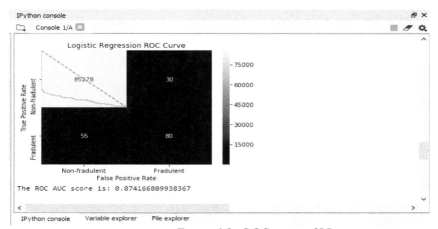

Figure 6.5 : ROC curve of LR

6.6. The AUPRC (Area Under the Precision-Recall Curve) shows the trade-off between precision and recall- As recall increases, precision plumets to a point that above 0.5 of recall precision is no better than an unskilled model, depicted by the 0.5 line.

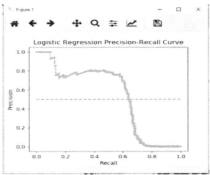

Figure 6.6 : Logistic Regression curve

25

6.7. Now we under sample the data. The idea behind under sampling in this case is creating a 50/50 ratio for class 1 (fraudulent) and class 0 (non-fraudulent), but randomly selecting a number of observations from the majority class (class 0 in this case) that equals that of the number of observations from the minority class (class 1). And apply logistic Regression algorithm.

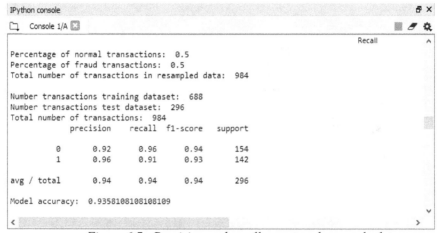

```
IPython console                                                          ⊟ ×
  Console 1/A                                                         ▨ 🖉 ⚙

                                                            Recall         ∧
Percentage of normal transactions:  0.5
Percentage of fraud transactions:  0.5
Total number of transactions in resampled data:  984

Number transactions training dataset:  688
Number transactions test dataset:  296
Total number of transactions:  984
             precision    recall  f1-score   support

          0       0.92      0.96      0.94       154
          1       0.96      0.91      0.93       142

avg / total       0.94      0.94      0.94       296

Model accuracy:  0.9358108108108109                                     ∨
<                                                                    >
```

Figure 6.7 : Precision and recall report under sample data

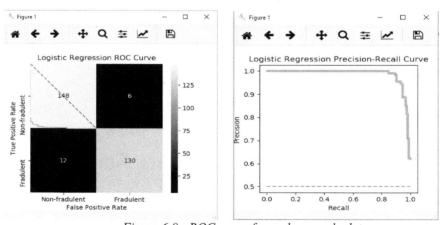

Figure 6.8 : ROC curve for under sample data

Precision for the detection of fraudulent transaction is now 0.92 and recall is 0.91, much better results than with the much larger but highly unbalanced set before. The ROC AUC score is- 0.9835833180903603. No huge trade-off between precision and recall but rather a similarly high rates for both precision and recall.

6.8. Now we perceive the outliers in order that we detect the anomalies. So as to boom the version accuracy. So Determine the number of fraud and legitimate transactions in the dataset. So then outlier fraction is zero.0017234102419808666 way that blunders is decrease. We apply 3 classifiers Isolation Forest, Local Outlier Factor and Support Vector Machine and predict the fraud rating.

```
  Anaconda Prompt - python finalsdesser.py
Isolation Forest: 73
Accuracy Score :
0.9974368877497279
Classification Report :
                 precision      recall    f1-score     support

             0       1.00        1.00        1.00       28432
             1       0.26        0.27        0.26          49

avg / total          1.00        1.00        1.00       28481

Local Outlier Factor: 97
Accuracy Score :
0.9965942207085425
Classification Report :
                 precision      recall    f1-score     support

             0       1.00        1.00        1.00       28432
             1       0.02        0.02        0.02          49

avg / total          1.00        1.00        1.00       28481

Support Vector Machine: 8516
Accuracy Score :
0.7009936448860644
Classification Report :
                 precision      recall    f1-score     support

             0       1.00        0.70        0.82       28432
             1       0.00        0.37        0.00          49

avg / total          1.00        0.70        0.82       28481

Scores: [0.0, 0.0, 0.6535947712418301, 0.0, 0.0]
loss : 0.131%
[INFO] starting training...
```

Figure 6.9 : Outlier Classification

It is determined that Isolation Forest detected seventy three errors versus Local Outlier Factor detecting 97 mistakes vs. SVM detecting 8516 errors. Isolation Forest has a 99.74% greater correct than LOF of 99.75% and SVM of 70.09%. When comparing blunders precision & do not forget for 3 models , the Isolation Forest accomplished lots higher than the LOF as we will see that the detection of fraud cases is round 27 % as opposed to LOF detection charge of just 2 % and SVM of 0%. So typical Isolation Forest Method carried out much better in determining the fraud cases that is around 30%.

6.9. Applying LR with Stochastic Gradient Descent-

```
Scores: [0.0, 0.0, 0.6535947712418301, 0.0, 0.0]
loss : 0.131%
[INFO] starting training...
```

Figure 6.10 : Loss in credit card transaction

It indicates that there is lack of 0.131% in transaction. And no error in epochs new release generation and mastering price. A ok cost of five turned into used for move- validation, giving each fold 768/5 = 153.6 or simply over a hundred and fifty records to be evaluated upon every generation. A mastering price of zero.1 and 100 schooling epochs have been chosen with a little experimentation.

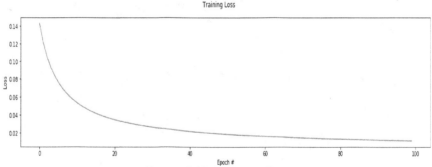

Figure 6.11 : Training loss

As the plot demonstrates, we're able to study a weight matrix W that efficaciously classifies each of the statistics points .I honestly have also protected a plot that visualizes loss decreasing in similarly iterations of the Stochastic Gradient Descent set of rules. So that means 0.13 % is a training loss manner accuracy of this model is 86%. At each generation loss cost decreases. If loss decreases accuracy increases.

7. CONCLUSION AND FUTURE SCOPE

In latest years, credit card usage has accelerated drastically. Fraud operations also are newly arriving in any other manner; there are greater techniques introduced to detect the frauds. The excellent way of credit card fraud is finding from the history of transactions; it predicts if the transaction is prison or fraudulent. A novel device getting to know method has been mentioned on this book for the detection of fraudulent transaction. This book is able to showcase the techniques and procedures applied in this technique. Benefits of enforcing such detection device will lessen the burden shouldered by means of the banks and users concerning the fraud. The techniques which have been studied right here, thru which credit card fraud can be detected quickly and rapid and the crime may be stopped.

REFERENCES

[1]. N. Malini, Dr. M .Pushpa, "Analysis on Credit Card Fraud Identification Techniques based on KNN and Outlier Detection", 3rd International Conference on Advances in Electrical, Electronics, Information, Communication and Bio- Informatics, Vol.5 Issue 5, pp 38-45, May 2017.

[2]. Pang-Ning Tan, Michael Steinbach, and Vipin Kumar. "Introduction to Data Mining," (First Edition). Addison-Wesley Longman Publishing Co., Inc., Boston MA, USA,2005

[3]. Sridhar Ramaswamy, Rajeev Rastogi, and Kyuseok Shim. "Efficient algorithms for mining outliers from large data sets". In ACM SIGMOD Record, Vol. 29.ACM, pp 427–438,2000

[4]. Varun Chandola, Arindam Banerjee, and Vipin Kumar. "Anomaly Detection- A Survey". ACM Computer. Survey. 41, 3, Article 15,July 2009,

[5]. Charu C Aggarwal and Saket Sathe. "Theoretical foundations and algorithms for outlier ensembles". ACM SIGKDD Explorations Newsletter 17, pp 24–47, 2015,

[6]. Arthur Zimek, Matthew Gaudet, Ricardo JGB Campello, and Jörg Sander. "Subsampling for efficient and effective unsupervised outlier detection ensembles". In Proceedings of the 19th ACM SIGKDD international conference on Knowledge discovery and data mining. ACM, pp 428–436. 2013.

[7]. Andrea Dal Pozzolo, Olivier Caelen, Reid A Johnson, and Gianluca Bontempi.. "Calibrating probability with under sampling for unbalanced classification". In Computational Intelligence, IEEE Symposium Series on. IEEE, pp 159–166, 2015.

[8]. Thomas G Dieterich. "Ensemble methods in machine learning". In International workshop on multiple classifier systems. Springer, pp 1–15,2000

[9]. Siddhartha Bhattacharyya, Sanjeev Jha, Kurian Tharakunnel, J. Christopher Westland, "Data mining for credit card fraud: A comparative study", Decision Support Systems 50 pp. 602–613,2011.

[10]. Suman and Nutan "Review paper on credit card fraud detection", International Journal of Computer Trends and Technology (IJCTT) – volume 4 Issue 7–July 2013.

[11]. Snehal Patilet al, "Credit Card Fraud Detection Using Decision Tree Induction Algorithm", International Journal of Computer Science and Mobile Computing, Vol.4 Issue.4, April- 2015.

[12]. Raghavendra Patidar, Lokesh Sharma, "Credit Card Fraud Detection Using Neural Network", International Journal of Soft Computing and

Engineering (IJSCE)ISSN: 2231-2307, Volume-1, Issue-NCAI2011, June 2011.

[13]. Yogesh Bharat Sonawane , Akshay Suresh Gadgil , Aniket Eknath More, Niranjan Kamalakar Jathar , "Credit Card Fraud Detection Using Clustering Based Approach", IJARIIE-ISSN(O)-2395-4396 Vol-2 Issue-6, 2016.

[14]. Mr.P. Matheswaran, Mrs.E.SivaSankari ME, Mr.R.Rajesh, "Fraud Detection in Credit Card Using Data Mining Techniques, Volume II, Issue I",IJRSET- February-2015.

[15]. K.RamaKalyani, D.UmaDevi, "Fraud Detection of Credit Card Payment System by Genetic Algorithm", International Journal of Scientific & Engineering Research Volume 3, Issue 7, July-2012.

[16]. Dr R.Dhanapal, Gayathiri.P, "Credit Card Fraud Detection Using Decision Tree For Tracing Email And Ip", IJCSI International Journal of Computer Science Issues, Vol. 9, Issue 5, No 2, September 2012.

[17]. Arthur Zimek, Ricardo JGB Campello, and Jörg Sander. "Ensembles for unsupervised outlier detection": challenges and research questions a position paper. Acm Sigkdd Explorations Newsletter 15, pp 11–22, 2014

[18]. Adrian Banarescu "Detecting and Preventing Fraud with Data Analytics", Elsevier, pp 1827-1836, 2015.

[19]. Aman Srivastava, Mugdha Yadav, Sandipani Basu, Shubham Salunkhe, Muzaffar Shabad "Credit Card Fraud Detection at Merchant Side using Neural Networks", 978-9-3805-4421-2, IEEE 2016.

[20]. S. Venkata Suryanarayana , G. N. Balaji , G. Venkateswara Rao "Machine Learning Approaches for Credit Card Fraud Detection" International Journal of Engineering & Technology, 7 (2) pp 917-920,2018

[21]. Frank E Grubbs. "Procedures for detecting outlying observations in samples". Techno metrics 11, pp 1–21. 1969.

[22]. Shivangi Sharma,Puneet Mitta,Geetika,"An Approach to Detect Credit Card Frauds using Attribute Selection and Ensemble Techniques", international Journal of Computer Applications, Volume 180, No. 21, pp 1-6, February 2018.

[23]. R. Mankame, S. Nikam and A. Gurav, "Using Data Mining Detection of Fraud in Transaction", International Journal of Engineering research Online, Vol. 5, No.2, pp.152-156, 2017

[24]. John O. Awoyemi, Adebayo O. Adetunmbi, Samuel A. Oluwadare, "Credit card fraud detection using Machine Learning Techniques: A Comparative Analysis", 2nd International conference on New IT trends, IEEE, pp 978-988, 2017.

[25]. B.Pushpalatha, C.Willson Joseph, "Credit Card Fraud Detection Based on the Transaction by Using Data mining Techniques", International Journal

of Innovative Research in Computer and Communication Engineering, Vol. 5, Issue 2, pp 1785-1794, February 2017.

[26]. You Dai, Jin Yan, Xiaoxin Tang, Han Zhao and Minyi Guo, "Online Credit Card Fraud Detection: A Hybrid Framework with Big Data Technologies", IEEE Trust Com/Big Data SE/ISPA, pp 1644-1653, 2016.

[27]. T Nuno Carneiroa, Gonc,alo Figueiraa, Miguel Costab, "A data mining based system for credit-card fraud detection in e-tail", Journal of DSS, pp 1-11, Sep 2016.

[28]. D. Viji, S. Kothbul Zeenath Banu, "An Improved Credit Card Fraud Detection Using K-Means Clustering Algorithm", International Journal of Engineering Science Invention (IJESI), One Day National Conference On "Internet Of Things The Current Trend In Connected World" NCIOT-2018, pp 59-64,2016

[29]. Abdallah,A.,Maarof, M. A., and Zainal,A. "A survey on Fraud detection system", 2016.

[30]. Ehramikar, S. "The Enhancement of Credit Card Fraud Detection Systems". Toronto, Canada: Master of Applied Science The-sis, University of Toronto. V. Vapnik. Statistical Learning Theory Wiley, New York, 2000

[31]. Sushmito Ghosh and Douglas L. Reilly, "Credit Card Fraud Detection with a Neural-Network" Proc. IEEE First Int. Conf. on Neural Networks, 2014.

[32]. Salvatore J. Stolfo, Wei Fan, WenkeLee, "Cost-based Modeling for Fraud and Intrusion Detection Results from the JAM Project", In Proceedings of the ACM SIGMOD Conference on Management of Data, pp 207–216, 2014.

[33]. Mohamed Hegazy, Ahmed adian, Mohamed Ragaie, "Enhanced Fraud Miner: Credit Card Fraud Detection using Clustering Data Mining Techniques", Egyptian Computer Science Journal (ISSN: 1110 – 2586) Volume 40 – Issue 03, September 2016

[34]. Priya Ravindra Shimpi, Prof. Vijayalaxmi Kadroli Angrish, "Survey on Credit Card Fraud Detection Techniques", International Journal Of Engineering And Computer Science ISSN: 2319-7242, 2012.

[35]. Neha Sethi, Anju Gera, April 2014, "A Revived Survey of Various Credit Card Fraud Detection Techniques", International Journal of Computer Science and Mobile Computing, IJCSMC, Vol. 3, Issue. 4, pp.780 – 791, April 2014.

[36]. Krishna Kumar Tripathi, Mahesh A. Pavaskar, "Survey on Credit Card Fraud Detection Methods", International Journal of Emerging Technology and Advanced Engineering, Vol 2, Issue 11, pp.721 – 726, November 2012.

[37]. Eswari.M,Navaneetha,Krishnan.M." Survey on Various Types of Credit Card Fraud and Security Measures", International Journal of Advanced Research in Computer Science and Software Engineering , Volume 4, Issue 1, pp.1235 – 1238, January 2014.

[38]. Anika Nahar, Sharmistha Roy, "A Survey on Different Approaches used for Credit Card Fraud Detection", International Journal of Applied Information Systems (IJAIS) Foundation of Computer Science FCS, New York, USA Volume 10 – No.4,pp.29 – 34, January 2016.

[39]. Priya Ravindra Shimpi, Prof. Vijayalaxmi Kadroli , "Survey on Credit Card Fraud Detection Techniques", International Journal Of Engineering And Computer Scienc, Volume 4 Issue 11, pp 15010-15015, Nov 2015.

Publisher: Eliva Press SRL

Email: info@elivapress.com

Eliva Press is an independent publishing house established for the publication and dissemination of academic works all over the world. Company provides high quality and professional service for all of our authors.

Our Services:
Free of charge, open-minded, eco-friendly, innovational.

-All services are free of charge for you as our author (manuscript review, step-by-step book preparation, publication, distribution, and marketing).
-No financial risk. The author is not obliged to pay any hidden fees for publication.
-Editors. Dedicated editors will assist step by step through the projects.
-Money paid to the author for every book sold. Up to 50% royalties guaranteed.
-ISBN (International Standard Book Number). We assign a unique ISBN to every Eliva Press book.
-Digital archive storage. Books will be available online for a long time. We don't need to have a stock of our titles. No unsold copies. Eliva Press uses environment friendly print on demand technology that limits the needs of publishing business. We care about environment and share these principles with our customers.
-Cover design. Cover art is designed by a professional designer.
-Worldwide distribution. We continue expanding our distribution channels to make sure that all readers have access to our books.

www.elivapress.com